SPACE JOBS

by Catherine C. Finan

BEARPORT
PUBLISHING

Minneapolis, Minnesota

Credits:
Cover, mnowicki/Shutterstock, IanDagnall Computing/Alamy, M.Aurelius/Shutterstock, Klever_ok/Shutterstock; Title Page, 4 top, 4 bottom, 5 top, 7 top, 10 bottom right, 11, 13 top, 14, 15 top right, 15 bottom right, 17 top, 18 bottom, 19 top, 19 bottom, 22 top, 23 top, 24 top, 25 top right, 25 top, 25 bottom, 27 middle, 27 bottom, NASA/Public Domain; 4 bottom left, MNBB Studio/Shutterstock; 4 bottom right, 5 top right, 9 top left, 21 bottom left, LightField Studios/Shutterstock; 5 middle left, NASA/JPL-Caltech/MSSS/Public Domain; 5 middle right, ESO/Yuri Beletsky/Creative Commons; 5 bottom left, Gorodenkoff/Shutterstock; 5 bottom right, ESA–C. Carreau/ATG medialab/Creative Commons; 6, ESO/B. Tafreshi (twanight.org)/Creative Commons; 6 bottom left, Prostock-studio/Shutterstock; 6 bottom middle, Astor57/Shutterstock; 6 bottom right, 10 top, 11 bottom middle, 12 bottom, Gorodenkoff/Shutterstock; 7 top right, 15 top, NASA/JPL/Public Domain; 7 middle, Chris Baynham/Shutterstock; 7 bottom, Eduard Ender/Public Domain; 7 bottom middle, dekazigzag/Shutterstock; 8, buradaki/Shutterstock; 8 bottom left, 8 bottom right, 27 top left, Design Projects/Shutterstock; 9 top, ESO/M. Zamani/Creative Commons; 9 (Collage images from NASA) Triff/Shutterstock; 9 bottom left, Halfpoint/Shutterstock; 9 bottom middle, Fab_1/Shutterstock; 9 bottom right, AF-Photography/Shutterstock; 11 bottom left, Nanette Dreyer/Shutterstock; 12 top, raigvi/Shutterstock; 12 bottom left, fizkes/Shutterstock; 13 bottom, Who is Danny/Shutterstock; 13 bottom left, Draper Laboratory; restored by Adam Cuerden/Public Domain; 13 bottom right, Dragon Images/Shutterstock; 15 bottom, 23 middle, 26 bottom, NASA/JPL-Caltech/Public Domain; 16, (EVA). PHOTOGRAPHER: Bill Brassard (NBL)/Creative Commons; 17 middle, Staff Sgt. Melanie Hutto, 6th Air Mobility Wing Photojournalist/Public Domain; 17 bottom left, NASA/Aubrey Gemignani/Creative Commons; 17 bottom right, NASA Photo/Tom Tschida/Public Domain; 18 top, 26 top, 27 top, SpaceX/Public Domain; 20–21 bottom, NASA/Robert Markowitz/Public Domain; 21 top left, Kim Shiflett/NASA/Public Domain; 21 top right, Marshall Space Flight Center/NASA/Public Domain; 22 bottom, 3Dstock/Shutterstock; 23 bottom, Levranii/Shutterstock; 23 bottom left, RossHelen/Shutterstock; 23 bottom right, tryton2011/Shutterstock; 24 bottom left, VaLiza/Shutterstock; 24 bottom right, Gelpi/Shutterstock; 25 bottom left, Juice Flair/Shutterstock; 27 bottom left, NASA/Aubrey Gemignani/Creative Commons; 28 top left, Jacob van Meurs/Public Domain; 28 bottom left, Justus Sustermans/Public Domain; 28 bottom middle, Be Good/Shutterstock; 28 middle, Kozak Sergii/Shutterstock; 28 bottom right, Nikola Bilic/Shutterstock; 28 bottom lower right, Banana Republic images/Shutterstock; 28–29, Austen Photography

President: Jen Jenson
Director of Product Development: Spencer Brinker
Senior Editor: Allison Juda
Associate Editor: Charly Haley
Designer: Elena Klinkner

Developed and produced for Bearport Publishing by BlueAppleWorks Inc.
Managing Editor for BlueAppleWorks: Melissa McClellan
Art Director: T.J. Choleva
Photo Research: Jane Reid

Library of Congress Cataloging-in-Publication Data

Names: Finan, Catherine C., 1972- author.
Title: Space jobs / by Catherine C. Finan.
Description: Minneapolis, Minnesota : Bearport Publishing, [2022] | Series: X-treme facts : space | Includes bibliographical references and index.
Identifiers: LCCN 2021039160 (print) | LCCN 2021039161 (ebook) | ISBN 9781636915104 (library binding) | ISBN 9781636915173 (paperback) | ISBN 9781636915241 (ebook)
Subjects: LCSH: Astronautics--Vocational guidance--Juvenile literature. | Space sciences--Vocational guidance--Juvenile literature.
Classification: LCC TL850 .F56 2022 (print) | LCC TL850 (ebook) | DDC 629.4023--dc23
LC record available at https://lccn.loc.gov/2021039160
LC ebook record available at https://lccn.loc.gov/2021039161

For more information, write to Bearport Publishing, 5357 Penn Avenue South, Minneapolis, MN 55419.
Printed in the United States of America.

Contents

Help Wanted!

Outer space is pretty amazing, right? There are planets, moons, and trillions of stars. Who knows what else might be out there? Maybe someday it'll be your job to find out! From astronauts to robotics **engineers**, lots of people are working in many different jobs to help us learn more about our solar system and the rest of the universe. Let's look at some of the coolest space jobs!

Aerospace engineers build machines **that travel into space.**

IT'S A BIG JOB, BUT SOMEONE'S GOTTA DO IT.

It takes a lot of people to **launch** a spacecraft and keep it running. Many of them do their jobs from Earth.

GOING TO SPACE STARTS RIGHT HERE ON THE GROUND.

WOW, YOU'RE SO DOWN-TO-EARTH!

Before astronauts travel to space, they scuba dive on Earth as part of their training.

WAIT, DOES THIS MEAN I HAVE TO GET MY SPACESUIT WET?!

Astronomers use powerful telescopes to discover stars, planets, and more!

Robotics engineers have designed vehicles that drive around on Mars and send information about the planet back to Earth.

Robotics engineers also make it possible to control unmanned spacecraft billions of miles from Earth.

YES, MA'AM!

NOW, MOVE TO THE LEFT!

Awesome Astronomers

Do you look up at the night sky and wonder what lies beyond Earth? Do you want to know more about how the universe was created? If so, a job as an astronomer might be for you. Astronomers are scientists who study outer space using telescopes, cameras, and computers. They track things in space—such as planets, moons, stars, and **galaxies**—to see how they move and change.

Astronomers have been studying the night sky for thousands of years. That makes astronomy the oldest space job!

WHOA! HOW DO I UPGRADE MY TELESCOPE TO MATCH THE BIG ONES?

OH, PLEASE! WE USED TO LOOK AT STARS WITH OUR BARE EYES, AND WE WERE JUST FINE!

Astronomers study space using huge **telescopes** at buildings called **observatories**.

The Keck Observatory in Hawaii has twin telescopes that are each 33 feet (10 m) wide!

Some astronomers use computers to make **models** that explain how things happen in outer space.

Astronomers use math to measure the huge distances between things that are very far away in space.

In 1543, astronomer Nicolaus Copernicus discovered that Earth moves around the sun. Before this, people thought Earth was the center of the universe!

COPERNICUS, ARE YOU SURE EARTH MOVES AROUND THE SUN?

SERIOUSLY, TRUST HIM ON THIS ONE.

YES, IT SAYS IT RIGHT HERE!

A New Era with Astrophysicists

Throughout history, astronomers have studied our sun, our moon, and the stars. They've tracked the movement of planets, **asteroids**, and **comets**. But advances in technology have led to a much newer branch of this ancient science. It's called astrophysics. Astrophysicists study the physical properties of things in space. Thanks to them, we now know what many space objects are made of, how they formed, and how they've changed over billions of years. Astrophysicists give us the far-out facts!

Astrophysicists look for signs of life on other planets and moons across the universe.

Astrophysicists use physics to learn about space. Physics is the science that studies light, heat, sound, electricity, and force.

IS ANYBODY OUT THERE?

I DON'T THINK THEY KNOW WHERE WE ARE.

MAYBE THEY'LL USE PHYSICS TO TRY TO FIND US.

Astrophysicists work with telescopes and computers. They also **have tools called spectrographs that help them study light from stars.**

IT CAN SEE THE LIGHT!

WHAT DOES THAT DO?

Astrophysicists study stars, including our sun, to better understand how stars are born and how they burn out and die.

Some astrophysicists use **chemistry** to figure out what planets and moons are made of.

OUR SUN IS SLOWLY BURNING OUT!

THIS IS SUCH A BUMMER! I'M GOING TO GO STUDY THE PLANETS AND MOONS INSTEAD.

YOU MEAN IT'S NOT GOING TO LIVE FOREVER?

Building Space Machines

The work of astronomers and astrophysicists would look totally different without the incredible machines designed by aerospace engineers. These machines include huge telescopes orbiting Earth that let us see far into space, as well as powerful spacecraft that we use to travel there! Machines built by aerospace engineers have allowed us to explore the universe in ways that used to be impossible.

I'M A GREAT PROBLEM SOLVER!

WHAT CAN I SAY? I LIKE TO STAY BUSY.

Aerospace engineers use computer models to be sure there are no problems before a spacecraft leaves Earth.

In 1969, Neil Armstrong became the first human to walk on the moon. But before he was an astronaut, he worked as an aerospace engineer and pilot.

The term *aerospace engineering* wasn't used until 1958—the same year **NASA** formed.

THANKS, AEROSPACE ENGINEERS! I'D BE NOTHING WITHOUT YOU.

Aerospace engineers worked on NASA's Space Launch System, also called the megarocket. This powerful rocket will bring astronauts to the moon for the first time since 1972!

Aerospace engineers also **design airplanes and military aircraft.**

I COULD, BUT I'D RATHER BE DESIGNING MORE ROCKETS!

HEY, COULD YOU MAKE ME AN AIRPLANE?

Compute This!

Aerospace engineers aren't the only ones who work on space machines. Whether it's a rocket or a space station, all spacecraft need complex computer equipment and programs. That's where computer engineers come in! Hardware engineers create equipment that gathers information both in space and from Earth. Software engineers make sure the machines' computer systems work well. That's a lot of computing!

Computer hardware engineers develop the physical parts of a computer, such as circuit boards and memory devices.

NOTHING'S GOING TO WORK WITHOUT ME!

Hardware engineers make models to test whether a device will work.

WHAT HAPPENS IF YOUR MODEL DOESN'T WORK?

WE'LL JUST BUILD A BETTER ONE!

Computer technology is always changing, so computer engineers must keep learning new things!

THE MORE THE MERRIER . . .

It takes more than 50 computers to run the International Space Station (ISS)—a lab that floats around Earth where astronauts live and work.

Software engineers help create computer programs and codes. Computers use these as instructions about how to work.

Computer engineer Margaret Hamilton led the software team that helped NASA send the first humans to the moon in 1969. Her team wrote 11,000 pages of code for the mission!

THIS IS THE CODE THAT GOT US TO THE MOON!

WOW! THIS STACK IS TALLER THAN ME!

Space Robots

And there is yet *another* type of engineering involved in the team effort to explore space! Robotics engineers use mechanical, electrical, and software engineering to design robots that work in space. These robots do things that would be dangerous for humans. Some robots repair the outside of the ISS. Others explore Mars's surface. Robots have even traveled outside our solar system!

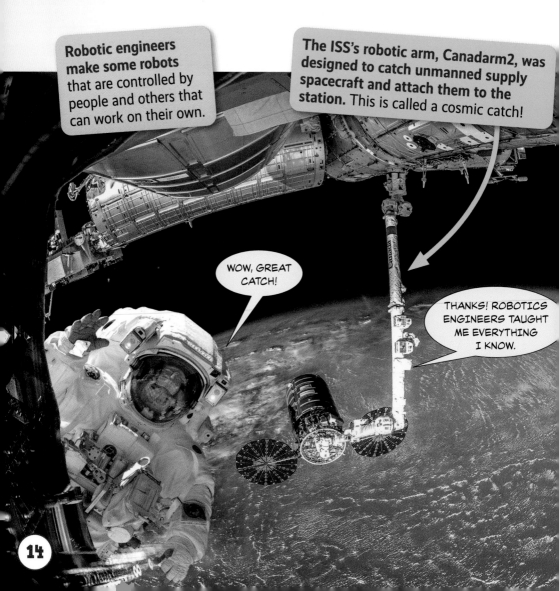

Robotic engineers make some robots that are controlled by people and others that can work on their own.

The ISS's robotic arm, Canadarm2, was designed to catch unmanned supply spacecraft and attach them to the station. This is called a cosmic catch!

WOW, GREAT CATCH!

THANKS! ROBOTICS ENGINEERS TAUGHT ME EVERYTHING I KNOW.

Space probes are robots that explore other planets, moons, and more. Robotics engineers design probes to operate on their own.

The space probe *Voyager 1* has left our solar system but continues to send information back to Earth. Robotics engineers helped make that possible.

The robotic **rover** *Perseverance* started exploring Mars in early 2021. Engineers designed the rover to plan its own routes.

Robotics engineers helped create the first unmanned space helicopter, *Ingenuity*. It made its first flight on Mars in April 2021.

So, You Want to Be an Astronaut?

While there are many jobs where people study space, only one job involves actually going there! Astronauts are people who travel beyond Earth's **atmosphere**. They have to be healthy enough to handle the physical stress that space puts on the human body. And as healthy as they are, they still need to go through hundreds of hours of training before going into space. Do you want to be an astronaut? Let's get started!

Scuba training in spacesuits prepares astronauts for dealing with low **gravity** while walking in space.

Many astronauts already have experience as jet pilots, but all astronauts must go through flight training.

HERE WE GO . . . WISH ME LUCK!

Astronauts must complete a water survival course, pass a difficult swimming test, and tread water for 10 minutes in a spacesuit!

Astronauts train in flight **simulations** to get used to the weightlessness experienced in space. **They might do it up to 40 times in one day!**

I THOUGHT WE WERE JUST GOING TO DO THE SIMULATION 39 TIMES TODAY . . .

I THINK I'M GOING TO BE SICK . . . AGAIN!

The aircraft used for astronaut training simulations **is called the vomit comet!**

Astronauts went on missions to the moon between 1969 and 1972. Since then, they've traveled only to space stations.

NASA plans to return to the moon by 2024, and future missions to Mars are being planned. Astronauts are training for these missions now!

I WILL TRAVEL TO MARS ONE DAY!

ARE YOU GOING TO JOIN HIM?

YES! I CAN'T WAIT TO START MY FLIGHT TRAINING!

Working in Space

Once astronauts make it through training, the real work begins! Today's astronauts head to the ISS, where they may live for months at a time. They keep the station running by checking equipment, making repairs, and cleaning—all while floating in low gravity. Astronauts also work on experiments that may one day help humans live on the moon or even Mars!

Astronauts go to space as part of a crew. Each person on the crew has a special job.

READY FOR THE FLIGHT?

YES, COMMANDER!

The crew's commander is responsible for everyone's safety. That's a big job!

Some astronauts pilot the spacecraft that travel from Earth to the ISS.

WHERE ARE YOU GOING? THE ISS IS TO THE LEFT.

I'M TAKING THE SCENIC ROUTE!

Astronauts must be brave to handle some of the risky work in space.

. . . BUT THE VIEW CAN'T BE BEAT!

IT'S A DANGEROUS JOB . . .

Astronauts go on spacewalks outside the ISS to check on equipment and make repairs.

Many astronauts have a background in science. They do science experiments while living on the ISS and send the information to Earth.

One thing astronauts study is their own bodies. And scientists on Earth do, too. **Sometimes, astronauts even send their poop to Earth for experiments!**

WHAT ARE WE SENDING DOWN TO EARTH?

YOU DON'T WANT TO KNOW!

Mission Control, Do You Read Me?

Astronauts may be the only people who work in space, but they always have backup on Earth. NASA astronauts work with Mission Control—the team of people on the ground that makes space travel possible. Spaceflights can't happen without people on Earth making sure that everything runs smoothly. Mission Control is constantly working to keep astronauts safe.

The Mission Control Center (MCC) at Johnson Space Center in Houston, Texas, **watches over the ISS and its crew 24 hours a day.**

SO, WHAT ARE THEY DOING TODAY?

SAME THING THEY WERE DOING YESTERDAY . . .

BORING!

MCC practices emergency **drills** with astronauts so everyone knows how to handle unexpected problems.

If MCC loses power because of bad weather, **workers at Marshall Space Flight Center in Huntsville, Alabama, take over.**

MCC even has a surgeon who watches over astronauts' health and gives medical advice if needed.

MCC's flight controllers make sure spacecraft systems are working correctly.

OPS PLANNER

PLUTO

When NASA landed people on the moon in 1969, **the average age of flight controllers was just 28 years old!**

SHHH, I'M BUSY LOOKING AFTER THE ISS!

I'M THE PERSON FOR THE JOB!

21

Brilliant Biologists

While Mission Control is busy keeping the ISS crew safe, biologists work with the astronauts on many experiments! Biologists are scientists who study living things. Through the experiments on the ISS, some biologists study how space affects living things. Others, called astrobiologists, use their knowledge of living things on Earth to try to figure out how life might exist on other planets. Biology can be out of this world!

Biologists study how plants grow on the ISS. This helps them figure out how space plants could be grown for food someday.

I CAN NEVER GROW SUCH NICE LETTUCE IN MY GARDEN ON EARTH!

I'LL GO PRETTY MUCH ANYWHERE.

Astrobiologists study simple life-forms such as bacteria and look for places in space where they might exist. Cool!

One ISS experiment studies tiny animals called tardigrades, which can live in extreme temperatures and survive years without water.

By studying the effects of space on astronauts' bodies, biologists learn how to help people stay healthy during long space journeys.

HAVE YOU EVER TRIED TO WORK OUT IN LOW GRAVITY? IT'S NOT EASY!

Astrobiologists are studying Jupiter's moon Europa. **They think things could live in an ocean beneath the moon's icy surface!**

Astrobiologists study animals that live in extreme environments on Earth. This helps them learn about living in extremes similar to space.

EASY! WE'RE LIKE ALIENS FROM EUROPA!

HOW DO YOU SURVIVE IN THAT ICY WATER?

An Odd Job?

From aerospace engineers to Mission Control, it takes many workers doing different jobs to send spacecraft, robots, and people into space. And there are many other space jobs that you've probably never thought about! Some people work to design spacesuits. And it's someone else's job to help astronauts get into those complicated suits. There's even a person whose job is to smell things before they're sent into space!

NASA has a chemical specialist who smells things to make sure nothing is sent to the ISS that could make the crew sick.

YES! ALL OF IT WAS SNIFFED BACK ON EARTH!

ARE YOU SURE THIS FOOD IS OKAY?

EWW! YOU WILL NEVER MAKE IT AS A NASALNAUT!

NASA's super sniffer is sometimes called a nasalnaut!

GREAT! PIZZA WITH ANCHOVIES. GRAB A SLICE!

Going on a spacewalk? Not without the perfect suit! **Spacesuit designers use science to make suits that keep astronauts safe.**

YOU'RE ALL SET TO GO, AND YOU'RE LOOKING SHARP!

Spacesuits are tricky to put on! Suit technicians help astronauts get into their suits and test all of the suits' technology.

Photographers work for NASA to capture historic moments in space exploration. Say cheese!

Space historians take care of items from space missions so we can see them at museums for a long time to come.

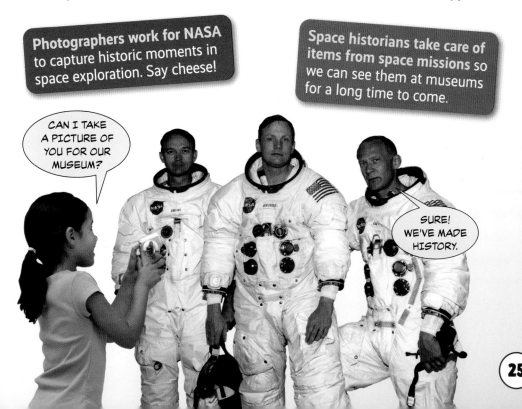

CAN I TAKE A PICTURE OF YOU FOR OUR MUSEUM?

SURE! WE'VE MADE HISTORY.

An Exciting Future

Space exploration has changed a lot over the years, and there's much more to come! In the future, people may live on the moon or Mars. And it used to be just a dream for people to travel to space for fun, but **private** spaceflight companies have made that dream possible. As more people travel to space or even live there, it will take more workers with space jobs to make it all happen. Will you have a space job someday?

A few people have already gone on short private trips to space, and companies are planning more. As more private spaceflights happen, more engineers will be needed to design spacecraft.

PILOTS WANTED!

More spaceflights means more pilots, too. Would you want to fly into space at more than 2,000 miles per hour (3,220 kph)?

People living in space someday will need water. **Mining** specialists might be able to gather water from asteroids. Wow!

So far, living on the moon has not been part of an astronaut's job—but NASA plans to change that! Astronauts will travel to the moon to test equipment for longer missions.

THEY'RE BACK!

HOW LONG DO YOU THINK THEY'RE STAYING?

SO, I GUESS WE LIVE HERE NOW.

Food engineers will be needed to make special foods that astronauts can keep in their spacecraft for very long missions.

Orange Ade

YOU COULD ALL BECOME ASTRONAUTS LIKE ME WHEN YOU GROW UP!

After the moon, the next goal is human travel to Mars. It will take many people working together to make that possible.

I WILL GO TO THE MOON!

I WANT TO BE THE FIRST ONE TO GO TO MARS!

Homemade Telescope
Craft Project

Hundreds of years before people figured out how to build machines to explore space, astronomers used simple telescopes to study the night sky. You can make your own telescope to do some space exploration on a clear night, just like an astronomer!

In 1608, Hans Lippershey made one of the first telescopes by putting two curved pieces of glass in a long tube.

What You Will Need

- 2 paper towel rolls
- Scissors
- Paints and a paintbrush
- Stickers
- Tape
- 2 convex lenses (You can get these from a pair of magnifying glasses or reading glasses—have an adult remove the lenses for you.)

The famous astronomer Galileo Galilei was the first person to use a telescope to explore the night sky.

Step One

Use scissors to cut one of the paper towel rolls down the side.

Step Two

Paint the rolls and leave them to dry. If you want, you can decorate the uncut roll with stickers.

Step Three

Insert the cut roll into the uncut roll. Make sure the cut roll can move easily inside the other roll. Tape the cut end together.

Step Four

Tape one lens to the inner roll with the curve facing inside. Tape the other lens to the outer roll with the curve facing outward. Hold the inner roll to your eye and focus by sliding the outer roll closer or farther away. Never point the telescope at the sun, and have fun!

Glossary

aerospace the space in Earth's atmosphere and beyond, as well as the scientific study of that space

asteroids rocks found in space

astronomers scientists who study space

atmosphere the gases surrounding a planet

chemistry the science that studies the basic elements and how they function

comets objects in space that are made up of dust and ice that sometimes form a long tail

drills training exercises that are repeated for practice

engineers people who design machines

galaxies collections of billions of stars and other matter held together by gravity

gravity the force that pulls things toward Earth, the sun, or other bodies in space

launch to send into the air with a lot of power

mining digging something out of rock or the ground

models small copies of something, often used to make the same thing in a larger size

NASA National Aeronautics and Space Administration; the United States' organization that conducts space travel and research

private owned by an individual person or company; not part of the government

rover a vehicle made for exploring the surface of a planet or moon

simulations things that seem like a certain experience

telescopes instruments that use lenses and mirrors to make distant objects appear larger

unmanned not carrying people

Read More

Owen, Ruth. *Space Robot Engineers (Thrilling Science and Technology Jobs)*. New York: AV2, 2020.

Rechner, Amy. *Astronaut (Torque: Cool Careers)*. Minneapolis: Bellwether Media, 2020.

Rose, Rachel. *Christina Koch: Astronaut and Engineer (Bearport Biographies)*. Minneapolis: Bearport Publishing, 2021.

Learn More Online

1. Go to **www.factsurfer.com** or scan the QR code below.

2. Enter **"Space Jobs"** into the search box.

3. Click on the cover of this book to see a list of websites.

Index

About the Author

Catherine C. Finan is a writer living in northeastern Pennsylvania. One of her most-prized possessions is a telescope that lets her peer into space.